902 82267

# I·N·S·I·D·E
# FRANCE

Ian James

Photography: Chris Fairclough

## Franklin Watts

London · New York · Sydney · Toronto

# CONTENTS

© 1988 Franklin Watts
12a Golden Square
London W1

Published in the USA by
Franklin Watts Inc.
387 Park Avenue South
New York, N.Y. 10016

Franklin Watts Australia
14 Mars Road
Lane Cove
NSW 2066

Design: Edward Kinsey
Illustrations: Hayward Art Group

UK ISBN: 0 86313 578-1
US ISBN: 0-531-10640-3
Library of Congress Catalog
Card Number: 88-50362

Phototypeset by Lineage Ltd, Watford
Printed in Belgium

Additional Photographs:
Mansell Collection 8; Popperfoto 9;
Kobal Collection 22 (B);
Phillips Collection 22 (T)

Front cover: Zefa
Back cover: Chris Fairclough

# The land

France is the largest country in Europe except for the Soviet Union. It is bordered by the English Channel in the northwest, the Bay of Biscay on the southwest, and the Mediterranean Sea on the southeast. The island of Corsica is also part of France.

Much of northern and western France is lowlying, though Brittany and Normandy are hilly. The main uplands are the Vosges Mountains in the northeast, the Jura mountains and the Alps in the southeast, and the Pyrenees in the southwest. Lying entirely in France is the *Massif Central* (Central Highlands). France's highest peak is Mont Blanc in the Alps. At 4,807 m (15,771 ft), it is the highest mountain in Western Europe.

Below: **Brittany is an attractive, hilly region in northwest France.**

Left: **The snowy Alps are in the southeast, along France's border with Italy.**

Below: **The Seine, France's best known river, flows through the city of Paris.**

France's longest river is the Loire. It is 1,010 km (628 miles) long. Other major rivers include the Somme and Seine in the north, the Garonne and Dordogne rivers in the southwest and the Rhône and Saône rivers, which flow into the Mediterranean Sea. The Rhône valley and the Mediterranean coast have hot, dry summers and mild, moist winters. The Mediterranean coast includes a popular tourist area, called the French Riviera. The independent territory of Monaco is also on the southeast coast.

Northern and western France have a mild climate with plenty of rain brought in by moist Atlantic winds. The climate becomes drier to the east. The northeast has hotter summers and colder winters than the northwest.

Above: **The French Riviera on the Mediterranean coast is one of Europe's leading resort areas.**

# The people and their history

France has a mixed population. Its language is based on Latin, but other languages are spoken. For example, the Basques and Catalans in the Pyrenees and the Bretons in Brittany have their own tongues. Some people in the northeast speak German.

Early settlers in France included Celtic peoples from central Europe. They arrived in about 1000 BC. The Romans took the area in between 58 and 51 BC. In AD 486, Germanic tribes, including the Franks, invaded the area. France got its name from the Franks. Later arrivals were Norse people, ancestors of the Normans.

France became a powerful monarchy in the Middle Ages. Under Louis XIV (1638-1715), the country was a great seat of culture.

Below: **King Louis XIV. During his reign France became a very powerful nation.**

Above: **Many aristocrats and French revolutionary leaders who became unpopular died on the guillotine.**

The monarchy was overthrown in the French Revolution (1789-1799) and a republic was set up. In the early 19th century, a brilliant general, Napoleon (1769-1821), conquered much of Europe. He made himself emperor in 1804, but he was finally defeated in 1815.

Prussia defeated France in 1870-1871 and Germany conquered France in World Wars I and II. In 1958, General Charles de Gaulle, the French leader in World War II, introduced a new Constitution. France is a republic, with a National Assembly and a Senate. The President is Head of State. He has wide powers and serves seven-year terms. Under President de Gaulle, most of France's overseas colonies became independent.

Above: **Napoleon at the Battle of Waterloo in 1815.**

Left: **General Charles de Gaulle was leader of the Free French forces. He led the Allied forces when they liberated Paris in 1944.**

# Towns and cities

France is one of the least densely populated countries in Europe. In parts of France, you can drive along country roads for hours without seeing a village.

In the 1940s farming employed far more people than it does today. Because farm machinery now does the work of many people, many former country people have moved into the cities and towns. About 73 out of every 100 people now live in towns and cities as compared with 67 per cent in 1965. The two largest cities are Paris, which with its suburbs is the largest urban area in Europe, and Lyon, on the junction of the Rhône and Saône rivers. These two cities have many businesses and industries.

Below: **A country area in southeastern France.**

Right: **The region around Lille is a major urban and industrial area.**

Below: **Many villages and small towns, such as Dinan in Brittany, have looked much the same for hundreds of years.**

Marseille is France's third largest city and its chief port. It was founded by Greek colonists about 2,600 years ago. The fourth largest city, Lille, is in the middle of a large manufacturing region near the Belgian border. The fifth largest city is the port of Bordeaux on the Gironde River, which flows into the Bay of Biscay. It exports famous wines which are also called Bordeaux.

Many of France's cities contain beautiful old buildings. Around the old central city areas are modern housing estates and large apartment blocks. Although the cities are changing in appearance, many villages look much the same as they did hundreds of years ago.

Above: **Marseille, the ancient seaport in southeastern France.**

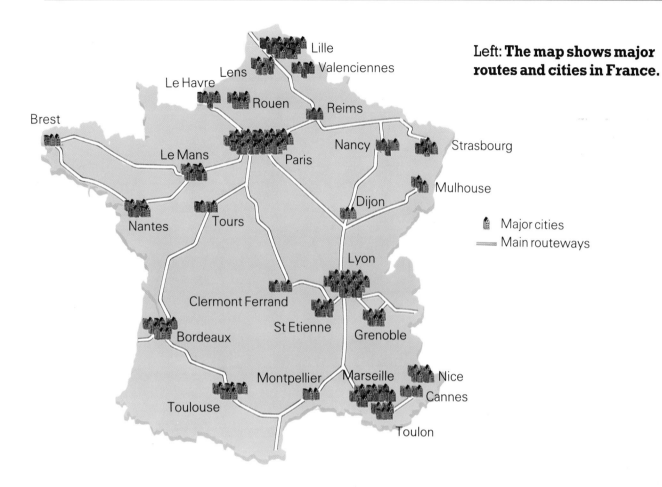

Left: **The map shows major routes and cities in France.**

Brest

Lille
Valenciennes
Lens
Le Havre
Rouen
Reims
Nancy
Strasbourg
Le Mans
Paris
Mulhouse
Dijon
Nantes
Tours
Lyon
Clermont Ferrand
St Etienne
Grenoble
Bordeaux
Montpellier
Marseille
Nice
Cannes
Toulouse
Toulon

▮ Major cities
══ Main routeways

Left: **A view of Paris showing the Eiffel Tower in the distance.**

13

Paris is one of the world's most beautiful cities. It was founded by a Celtic tribe called the Parisii, who built a settlement on an island in the River Seine. This island, called the Ile de la Cité, is now in the heart of Paris. On it stands the great Cathedral of Notre Dame, which was begun in 1163.

Paris contains many other impressive buildings, monuments, parks, elegant avenues, called *boulevards*, fine hotels, shops and restaurants. Landmarks include the Eiffel Tower, which rises 320m (1,050ft), and the Arc de Triomphe, a monument at the head of the tree-lined avenue called the Champs Elysées. The City has one of the world's finest art galleries, called the Louvre. Its Opera House, the Elysée palace (the official residence of the French President) and the Church of Sacré-Coeur attract tourists. Paris has an excellent *Métro* (underground railway system).

Below: **A plan of central Paris**
1 **Chaillot Palace**
2 **Eiffel Tower**
3 **Arc de Triomphe**
4 **Invalides**
5 **Place de la Concorde**
6 **Opera**
7 **The Louvre**
8 **Sacré-Coeur**
9 **The Bourse (Stock Exchange)**
10 **Luxembourg Palace**
11 **Panthéon**
12 **Notre Dame**
13 **Pompidou Centre**

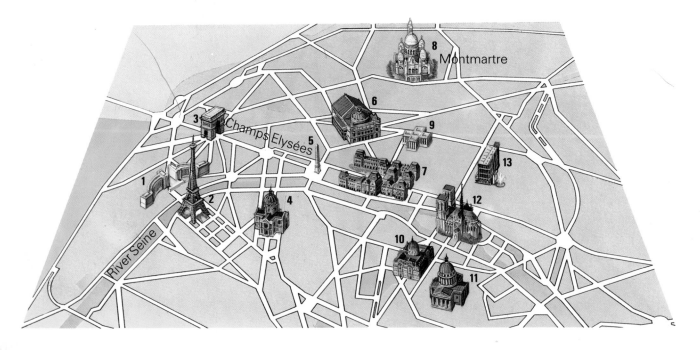

# Family Life

About half of French families own their home. About 54 per cent live in houses and 46 per cent in apartments, many of which are rented. Most homes are modern, but some in country areas still lack such things as electricity.

The family plays an important part in French life. In the past, grandparents, parents and children all lived together. In recent years, family units have become smaller. More and more people set up their own home, when they marry. However, family ties remain strong. Parents like to see a lot of their children. Mealtimes are special occasions for French people. Families gather together not only to eat, but to exchange news.

Below: **A French family outside their house in La Rochelle on the Atlantic coast.**

Left: **Many people live in well designed, modern apartments.**

Below: **Many families grow vegetables in their gardens.**

# Food

The French are famed for their *cuisine*, or cooking. Most French people are demanding shoppers. Many small shops sell only one kind of product. *Boulangeries* sell only bread. *Charcuteries* sell only cooked meats.

Breakfast usually consists of coffee, with bread or pastries. Lunch is the main meal of the day, while dinner is a lighter meal. The French are known for their soups, salads and sauces, often containing garlic, which accompany meat. Their excellent wines and cheeses are exported and enjoyed in many other countries. Famous French dishes include snails, onion soup, omelettes with herbs, various sea foods, including *bouillabaisse* (Mediterranean fish stew) and casseroles, such as *coq au vin* (chicken in red wine).

Below: **A stall selling cooked meats and sausages in Paris.**

Above: **Wine is drunk with most meals.**

Left: **The French take pride in presentation as well as preparation of food.**

# Sports and pastimes

Soccer is the most popular team sport in France. Shooting, fishing and motor racing are popular, but the Tour de France cycle race is perhaps the best known event. It covers about 4,000 km (2,500 miles) and lasts for about three weeks. *Boules* is a famous traditional game.

Watching television is a major pastime and 91 per cent of French households have a television set. Nearly half of the people read a newspaper every day.

In August, many work places close down for an annual vacation. Two out of every five families go to the seaside. Many people like sporting activity such as sailing and skiing. Other outdoor activities include climbing, walking and camping.

Below: **Cycling is a leading sport and form of exercise.**

Above: **Les Sables-d'Olonne, a resort on the Bay of Biscay.**

Left: **The traditional French game of boules can be played on any flat piece of ground.**

# The arts

France has produced many outstanding people in all the arts. In architecture, France has many great cathedrals, including those at Amiens, Chartres and Reims. The Loire valley contains magnificent *châteaux* (castles).

Such painters as Pierre Auguste Renoir (1841-1919) and Claude Monet (1840-1926) created many masterpieces. They belonged to the Impressionist group. They got this name because they tried to create an immediate impression of their subject.

French writers include Victor Hugo (1802-85), who wrote *Les Miserables*, Honoré de Balzac (1799-1850), who wrote *Eugénie Grandet*, and Emile Zola (1840-1902), author of *Germinal*. Composers include Georges Bizet (1838-75) and Claude Debussy (1862-1918).

Below: **The Cathedral of Notre Dame in Amiens is the largest church in northern France.**

Above: ***The Luncheon of the Boating Party*** is a work by Auguste Renoir, a great Impressionist painter.

Left: ***The Hunchback of Notre Dame*** by Victor Hugo was made into a successful movie.

# Farming

France is a prosperous industrial nation. But its leading natural resource is its soil. More than four-fifths of the land is used to produce crops, timber, or pasture for cattle and other animals.

Farming now employs about 9 per cent of all working people, as compared with 30 per cent in the late 1940s. Two-thirds of French farm income comes from meat and dairy products. The leading meat animals are beef cattle, followed by sheep. Milk, butter and cheese are major products. Famous French cheeses include Brie, Camembert and Roquefort.

The leading crop is wheat, followed by barley, maize, suger-beet and potatoes. Grapes are grown for making wine. Famous French wines include Beaujolais, Burgundy and Sauternes.

Below: **Animals are still used for transportation in some parts of France.**

Above: **A vineyard in southeastern France.**

Left: **A cheese stall in Rennes in Brittany.**

# Industry

France produces iron ore, bauxite, potash and coal. It also has coalfields and oilfields, but they do not produce enough for the country's needs. France must therefore import both of these fuels. About a quarter of France's electricity supply comes from hydroelectric stations, including the world's only tidal power station, while nearly half comes from nuclear power stations.

France is one of the world's leading industrial countries. Industries employ about 35 per cent of the workforce. France's chief exports are machinery, chemicals, cars, military equipment, fashion goods, food and wines, and iron steel. Exports and imports are usually roughly equal in value. Money also comes from foreign investments and tourism.

Below: **France is one of western Europe's chief car manufacturers.**

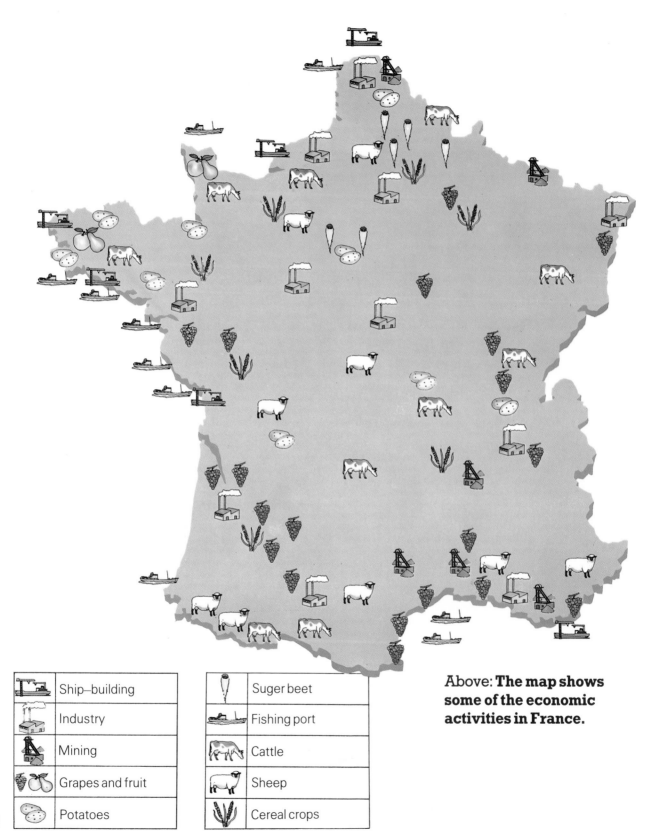

| | | | | |
|---|---|---|---|---|
| | Ship–building | | | Suger beet |
| | Industry | | | Fishing port |
| | Mining | | | Cattle |
| | Grapes and fruit | | | Sheep |
| | Potatoes | | | Cereal crops |

**Above: The map shows some of the economic activities in France.**

Much of the steel produced in France is used to make machinery, home appliances, such as refrigerators, and cars. Well-known vehicle making companies include Renault and Peugeot-Talbot-Citroën. France has large aircraft and chemical industries, while traditional tapestry, glass and pottery industries still flourish.

France leads the world in the perfume and fashion industries. Perfume is especially important in the south, where farmers grow the flowers used to make it. Paris is the heart of the French fashion industry. Every year, the designs of such fashion houses as Cardin, Dior and Yves St. Laurent influence the styles of clothes around the world.

Below: **French fashion has a great influence on clothes styles around the world.**

# Looking to the future

Many young men were killed in World Wars I and II and about four-fifths of the country's industries were destroyed between 1939 and 1945. In the late 1940s, France faced political and economic problems at home, while costly wars broke out in some of France's colonies.

In 1957, France became a founding member of the European Economic Community (EEC). Through the EEC, France worked to rebuild its economy. In 1958, President de Gaulle introduced a new Constitution, which gave France political stability. De Gaulle also made most of France's colonies independent, though the country still has four overseas departments (Guadeloupe, French Guiana, Martinique and Réunion), and some island territories.

Below: **The parents of many children in France originally came from France's colonies.**

France recovered quickly in the 1960s and today it is one of the world's richest and most successful industrial powers. Its success is based partly on hard work. This begins in school but it continues into adult life. The French work longer hours than Americans, Britons or West Germans. However, France faces some problems. The decline of old industries and the setting up of new, high-technology industries have caused unemployment.

France remains important in world affairs and its culture continues to have considerable influence. French is the official language in 20 countries besides France itself. It is spoken by more than 110 million people and is one of the world's major business languages.

Above: **This solar furnace is an example of France's many impressive achievements in technology.**

29

# Facts about France

**Area:**
547,026 sq km
(211,208 sq miles)

**Population:**
55,596,000

**Capital:**
Paris

**Largest cities:**
(Populations include
cities and suburbs)
Paris (8,707,000)
Lyon (1,221,000)
Marseille (1,111,000)
Lille (936,000)
Bordeaux (640,000)

**Official language:**
French

**Religion:**
Christianity

**Main exports:**
Machinery and
transportation
equipment, chemicals,
food and farm products

**Unit of currency:**
Franc

## France compared with some other countries

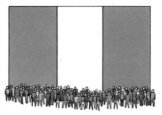
**France** 100 per sq. km.

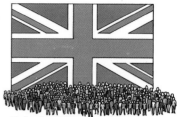
**Britain** 232 per sq. km.

**Australia** 2 per sq. km.

**USA** 26 per sq. km.

Above: **How many people?
France is less heavily
populated than most
European countries.**

Below: **How large? France
is large in European terms
but much smaller than the
United States or Australia.**

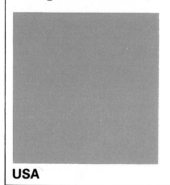
USA

Australia

France    UK

Below: **Some French money
and stamps. The franc is
divided into 100 centimes.**

WALES

ENGLAND

*North Sea*

*Strait of Dover*

*English Channel*

BELGIUM

W. GERMANY

Dunkerque
Calais
Boulogne
Lens
Lille
Douai
Valenciennes

LUXEMBOURG

Channel Is.
(UK)

Cherbourg

Dieppe

*R. Somme*

Amiens

Le Havre

Rouen

PICARDY

Reims

Metz

LORRAINE

Caen

NORMANDY

*R. Seine*

Paris

Versailles

CHAMPAGNE

Nancy

Strasbourg

Brest

BRITTANY

Rennes

Chartres

Fontainebleau

*R. Seine*

Chablis

*Vosges*

ALSACE

Lorient

Le Mans

Orléans

Mulhouse

St. Nazaire

Angers

ANJOU

Nantes

Tours

*R. Loire*

Bourges

Nevers

BURGUNDY

Dijon

*R. Vienne*

Poitiers

*R. Loire*

*R. Saône*

*Jura Mts.*

SWITZERLAND

La Rochelle

Rochefort

*Bay of Biscay*

Limoges

Roanne

Clermont
Ferrand

St. Etienne

Lyon

Mont Blanc
4807m

*Alps*

Grenoble

ITALY

AQUITAINE

*R. Dordogne*

*Massif
Central*

Bordeaux

*R. Garonne*

*Cévennes*

*R. Rhône*

*Alps*

GASCONY

Bayonne

Pau

Toulouse

Nîmes

Avignon

Arles

PROVENCE

MONACO

Nice

Lourdes

Montpellier

LANGUEDOC

Cannes

St Tropez

Marseille

Bastia

*Pyrénées*

ANDORRA

Toulon

SPAIN

Perpignan

*Mediterranean Sea*

Ajaccio

Bonifacio

Scale 1:5,000,000

0   20   40   60   80 miles

0    40    80    120 km

# Index